The Christian
Conservative
Coloring Book

For more information please address:

Garrett County Press

www.gcpress.com

Garrett County Press First Edition 2008

ISBN: 978-1-891053-09-2

BIOGRAPHICAL DATA

Kevin Stone graduated with honors from Pratt Institute in 1994. He has been published in numerous periodicals and books. He lived in the shadow of Sing Sing prison in New York where he toiled on his "maifesto" that will some day change the world. More of his work can be viewed at www.kstonedesign.com

Mackie Blanton, Ph.D., a pro bono Associate of the Gestalt Psychotherapy Institute of New Orleans/New York (1983 to Present), is currently a Senior Fulbright Lecturer at Ege Universitesi, Izmir, Turkey (2005-2007) in Contemporary Cultural and Literary Critical Theory. In 1987, he received a Fulbright Lectureship to Casablanca, Morocco, where he taught linguistics at the Ben M'Sik campus of Hassan II University.

From 1998 to 2005, he produced and hosted a public-access television show, Diversity on Common Ground, for New Orleans Access Television (NOATV) on public, educational, and governmental issues, for which he won, in 2000, a Pegasus Award for overall Excellence for Best Weekly Show of the Year and a second Pegasus Award for Best Producer of the Year.

In 2005 (before Hurricane Katrina), he retired as an Associate Professor of Linguistics in the Department of English, of the University of New Orleans, where he also served as the Associate Dean of Student Life for Multicultural Affairs.

He has written essays in linguistics, poetics, scientific and technical discourse, Louisiana dialects, Gestalt Psychotherapy, and Sufi and Hasidic sacred language. His current research is on the relationship of critical theory linguistics to sacriture, i.e., to the study of the practice of and the study of sacred discourse as a literary genre.

Printed on acid-free paper

The Christian Conservative Coloring Book

By Kevin Stone

Additional Commentary By Mackie Blanton

ILLUSTRATED BY KEVIN STONE

ADDITIONAL COMMENTARY BY MACKIE BLANTON

GARRETT COUNTY PRESS

For my father, William S. Stone,
who will go to his grave convinced that
the CIA killed Kennedy, the moon landing was staged
*and George W. Bush stole not one, but **two** elections.*

Did You Know...

"...that Pat Robertson, through rigorous training, leg-pressed 2,000 pounds?"
—*The Christian Broadcasting Network Website**

* Clay Travis of CBS SportsLine reported that the all-time Florida State University leg press record is held by Dan Kendra. He pressed 665 pounds. When Kendra broke the record the capillaries in his eyes burst.

"It doesn't say anywhere in the Constitution this idea of the separation of church and state."
— *Sean Hannity, August 25, 2003*

"I heard Satan say, 'Jesus is playing you for a sucker, Robertson.'"
— Pat Robertson, December 27, 1987

"...it is probable that 75 to 80 percent of the illnesses in the United States are psychosomatic."
— Pat Robertson, January 1, 1984

"I do not need to explain why I say things. That's the interesting thing about being the president. Maybe somebody needs to explain to me why they say something, but I don't feel I owe anybody an explanation."
— *President George W. Bush to Bob Woodward*

"Even if Bush stumbles and messes up — and he's had his share of stumbles and gaffes — I just think God's blessing is on him."
— *Pat Robertson*

"[I]f he thinks we're trying to assassinate him, I think that we really ought to go ahead and do it. It's a whole lot cheaper than starting a war."
— *Pat Robertson on Venezuelan President Hugo Chavez, Aug. 22, 2005*

"You say you're supposed to be nice to the Episcopalians and
the Presbyterians and the Methodists and this, that, and the other thing.
Nonsense, I don't have to be nice to the spirit of the Antichrist."
— Pat Robertson, January 14, 1991

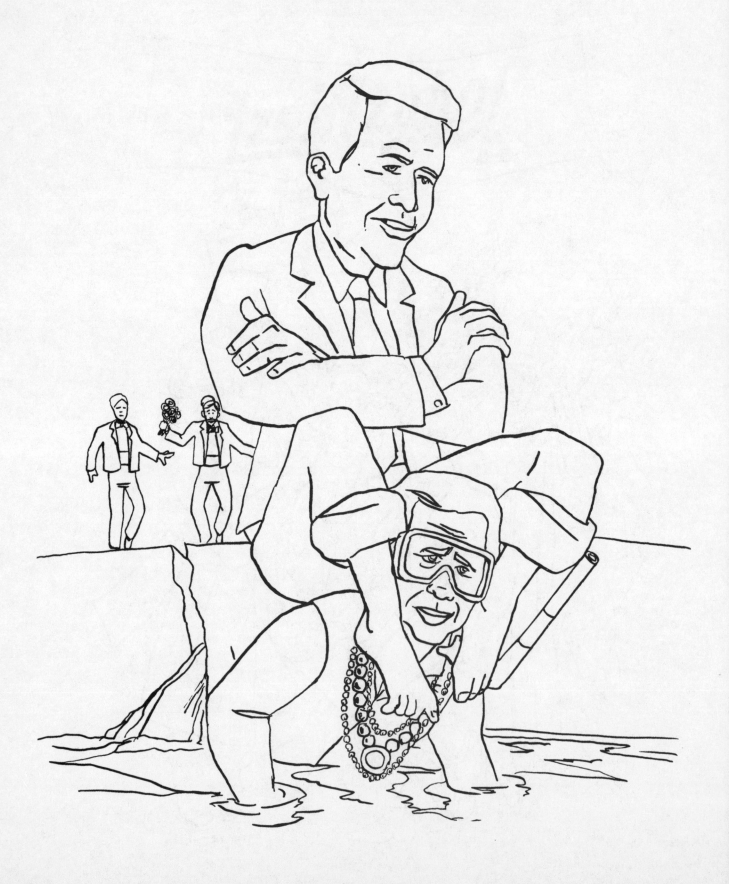

"I don't believe there's any issue that's more important than this one [the constitutional amendment banning gay marriage]."
— *Louisiana Sen. David Vitter, June 7, 2006*

"I had deep misgivings about this war, deep misgivings. And I was trying to say, Mr. President, you better prepare the American people for casualties. [But George W. Bush said:] 'Oh no, we're not going to have any casualties.'"
— *Pat Robertson, October 19, 2004*

"If I heard the Lord right about 2006, the coasts of America will be lashed by storms. There well may be something as bad as a tsunami in the Pacific Northwest."
— Pat Robertson, Jan 22, 1995

"Christ is the head of the household and the husband is the head of the wife, and that's the way it is, period."[1]
— Pat Robertson, 1995

[1]See "The Ordained, Disdained Vagina" by Mackie Blanton, on the second to last page.

"That [separation of church and state] was never in the Constitution. However much the liberals laugh at me for saying it, they know good and well it was never in the Constitution. Such language only appeared in the constitution of the communist Soviet Union."
— *Pat Robertson, Jan 22, 1995*

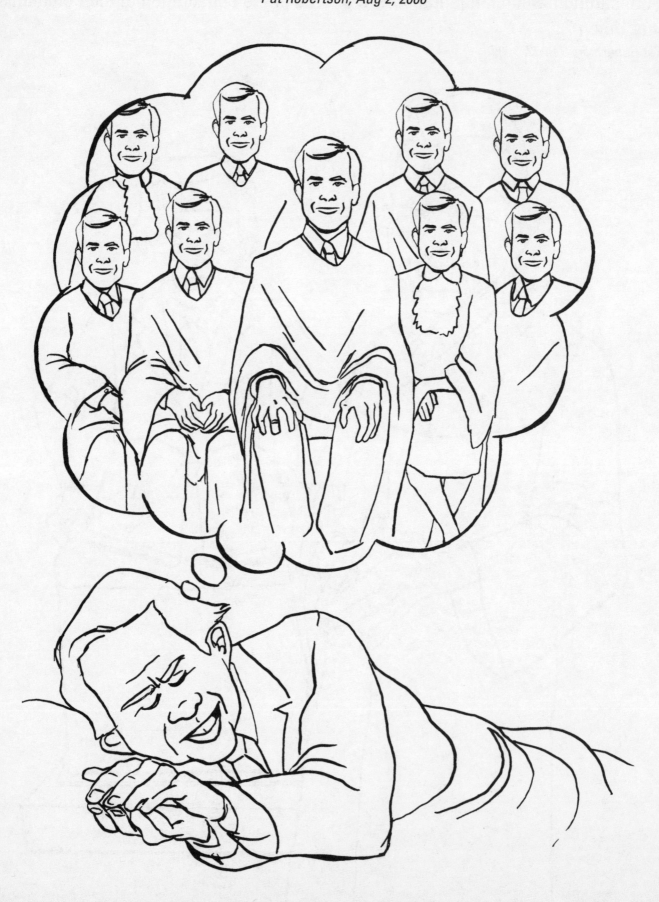

"The Antarctica ice is actually increasing. This -– just this hysteric global warming is unsupportable by facts."

— Rush Limbaugh, May 22, 2006

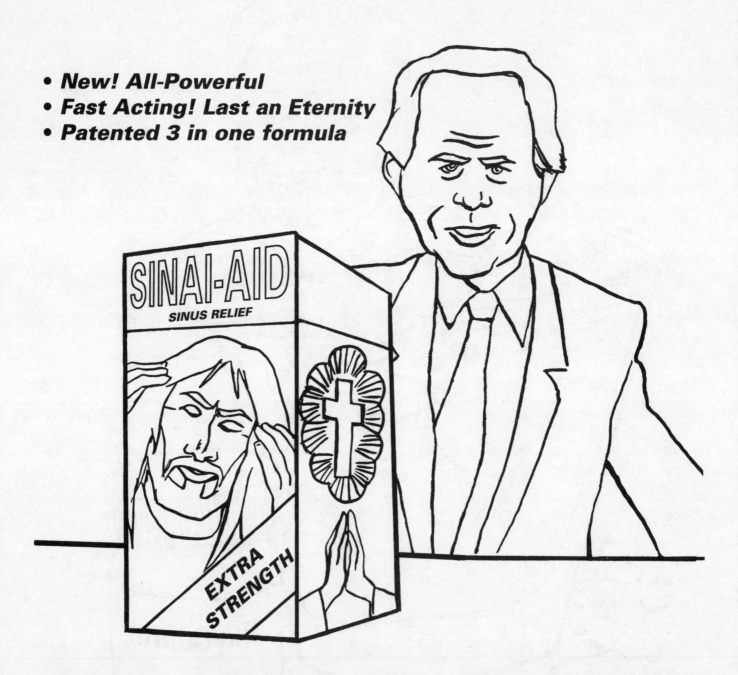

"I would like to ask the proponents of gay marriage — which violates, after all, traditions going back through all of human history — to now absolutely, positively guarantee that the next movement is not going to be allowing people to marry their pet horse, dog or cat."
—*Daniel Henninger of* The Wall Street Journal, *June 10, 2006*

"Homosexuals are not monogamous. They want to destroy the institution of marriage. It will destroy marriage. It will destroy the Earth."
— *James Dobson, October 23, 2004*

"But why should we hear about body bags, and deaths ... Or, I mean, it's, it's not relevant. So, why should I waste my beautiful mind on something like that?"
— *Barbara Bush, March 18, 2003*

"I think God's will has to be done in unifying people and companies to get that gas line built, so pray for that."

—Sarah Palin, June 2008
On building a $30 billion natural gas pipeline in Alaska

"If you go all the way back to the days following creation, men lived 900 years or more. I wonder if, when the millennium comes and there is no more sin on earth, people will once again live 200 or 300 years, or even longer."
— *Pat Robertson, , January 1, 1984*

The Ordained, Disdained Vagina

We have been led by its Patriarchs over the long life of monotheism to believe that tolerance is always only the tolerance of a necessary evil, or is always only the begrudging acceptance of another's way of being, or the resentful acceptance in our midst of another's merely being. In its gestures and designs, tolerance, by the insistent presence of intolerance — its hot-bloodied, sometimes genocidal boisterous lack — always seems lukewarm, or to be merely mewling and puking at the edge of human affairs. And what is lukewarm to the taste, like snot and puke, we want to quickly spit out; especially when it's the tepid, galling, gagging taste of others' beliefs.

This, in fact, is one of Jesus' cautions. Proclaiming that he had come to fulfill and to complete the 613 commandments of the Jewish Faith and Creed, Jesus also frightened the heart and mind of those who believed themselves willing to become his followers with the warning that he would, for all time, spit them out if ever they were to backslide, to become luke-warm. Christians are bound by this single fear and are therefore molded by the maw of intolerance.

Tolerance is therefore more elusive to us, more amorphous, more ephemeral, more effete; mealy-mouthed also, and temporizing. Jesus' cautionary teachings, admonitions, injunctions, and enjoinments, all of them, of course, are rooted as rewards and punishments in the initial existential promise of the God of the Jews, which anyone can plainly discern by attentively reading the first five books of the Tanakh, which are also the first five books of the Christian Bible. These verses also have their parallel in multiple verses of the Muslim's Al-Qur'an. Singularly

stated, the promise may be reiterated this way: Root out and rout out your enemy, who is My enemy, and you will be My People forever! This is what the Voice of the covenant of these verses of these Scriptures promise, so goes the traditional interpretation of all three faith communities. Morally self-righteous interpreters therefore have yet to put aside the negative, interpretive enjoinment of these verses.

In this Voice of the Text, however, is the hint of the root of the real problem. For Scripture — these three books, each originating a separate faith — is not the problem. Political, social, moral, and ideological interest is. Priests and mullahs, rabbis and ministers alike, have often invoked divine revelation to justify imperialism, forced conversions, colonialization, invasion, and centralized government. Tolerance, the outcome of so much solipsistic fart-threading, is therefore a sham, a feigned slant, a subtle subversion, and a dissembling stance. Hence, we have been taught by the monotheistic faiths to conclude that tolerance is the tolerance of a necessary evil: of the unenlightened evil inherent in the ways of others who do not hold to our faith and of the temporary, promissory evil in ourselves, in the ways that we must choose to transform others or to rout them out from our midst.

It is as if Heaven has forced us to find on our own the reality of tolerance through the growth of our knowledge of tolerance, as if tolerance can only indwell in us as intolerance evaporates from our demonic brain stem. One proof of this is that members of the monotheistic faiths see plainly the intolerance in the holy discourse of others' verses, but not the intolerance in the interpretation of their own. One's own Canon is the Voice of God, while that of others is the Voice of Satan. I wouldn't put it past the Heaven guiding our Patriarchs, be they rebbes, bishops, or sheiks, for setting us off on this journey in the first place, as if we first had to trek through the dark forests of our own nature in order to arrive at the Garden of Tolerance, presumably that very garden we first lost, the Garden of Eden.

So intolerance it is. So be it.

The thing about tolerance, in intolerance's pietistic skin, is that it is wholly patriarchal and hypocritical — and cunt-befuddled. Knotted in the very fabric of his language on the proper way to live a religiously correct life, and on the call for tolerance, are the fundamentalist preacher's literal-minded, a-historical, non-canonical harangues about moral decency and the proper family life.

Fearful of woman's vagina, and when they are not claiming that theirs is the one, true faith, these preachers reduce morality to an ideology about women's chastity. Protecting women's modesty and chastity predates monotheism, stemming from pre-Islamic, pre-Christian, and pre-Jewish traditional societies' bonds of kinship and family. Women's chastity is seen to be threatened always by what is contemporary to every age — the incursion of outside forces: innovations in male-female relationship rituals, in public-private displays of emotions and affection, in education, and in employment practices.

After all, throughout human history, a code of conduct and good taste has always been related as and practiced as a gentlemanly code. And the female has been both the ordained receiver and the disdained victim. As a victim of male strife, a woman is no different from one who is outside of the religious community.

America has mostly lost its tradition of the extended family, and it is mostly the fundamentalist, religiously moral communities that desire to bring back the extended family as it was first fashioned before the rise of the nation-state and the city. In traditional societies, or in traditional communities of democratic societies, the family has always been the basic economic unit. Traditionally, the extended family, across approximately three to four generations, has included the families of brothers and other close male relatives. The woman always joins another's household. Women in these societies or communities, as the wife and mother of a male So-and-So, have always had to give, and to give up, so much more than men: their name, their family, their village, their intellect, their daydreams, education, and, ultimately, their identity. In most such cases, the mother-in-law of the joined household never treats the new woman as a full member of her own family. The male, free to journey, is the released, outside insider; the female, never wholly free to exist outside of her body, is always the enclosed, inside outsider.

Women of such societies and communities over time are socially constructed to uphold and to maintain norms of religious tradition, or risk losing their lives, which is why it is always difficult to transform such communities toward modernity. The entire community checks the female's every move, beginning with her puberty, whose oncoming is signaled by the fact that she, as a pubic presence now, is removed from public sight to the inside of the house and is no longer allowed to play with boys. Family ties of the traditional extended family will usually prove to be stronger than egalitarian precepts, human rights principles, and inter-religious unity.

We've no reason to believe that women created such a ritualistic tradition among human societies, though they keep it going. We suspect that it was the male ego that did. The male's self-absorbed undeveloped ego and his sense of self-identity are so tied to his genitalia, and not to his humanness, that males unconsciously believe that they cannot be male without controlling the female. Male strife is always lived and relived on the backs of others.

Males fear the female's chromosomal, spiritual complexity. The self-righteousness and man-made superiority of the religiously moral male, especially, suggest that this is the case to hand. Men are most afraid of women's sexuality, which, I will suggest, is a projection and transference of their own involuntary sexual drives toward dominance over the female. While the close corners of the extended family assist women in unwittingly keeping their own lives in check, religion assists men in enclosing a moral moat around the family fortress.

Female sexuality naturally left to itself is and can be a part of so much more than the creation of male strife or of the neuroses of the enclosed vagina. The religiously moral ideology about the defilement of women's chastity, self-righteously preached obviously by men and ironically by women, suggests a deep-tissue fear of each woman's free control over her own body: a fear that she would be able to decide when to have sex, when to make love, when to have children, when to go for walks or journeys alone. In unreflective religious societies of today, like those of yesterday, women's lives are taken away just from the mere hint of pre-marital sex, rape, or a suspected wayward flirtatious glance.

Is America on its way to becoming an intolerant nation of cunt-befuddled fart-threaders

Mackie Blanton Kafl, Antalya, Turkey 27 July 2006 The Hotel Hadrian

NOTES ON THE QUOTES

1. "Did you know that Pat Robertston..."
Source: The Christian Broadcasting Network website (www.cbn.com). The claim of leg-pressing prowess was made in a story about Pat Robertson's Age-Defying Shake, which is filled with "energy-producing nutrients." The fact about Dan Kendra came from a May 22, 2006 cbs.sportsline.com story ("ClayNation: Pat Robertson's magical protein shake," by Clay Travis).

2. "It doesn't say..."
Sean Hannity proclaimed this anti-historical anti-fact on the 8/25/03 edition of "Hannity and Colmes." Source: http://www.americanprogress.org/issues/kfiles/b91585.html

3. "I heard Satan say..."
United Press International reported this line in the December 28, 1987 story, "Only Devout Christians or Jews Qualified." "Robertson had a conversation with Satan in 1960 at the time of his religious conversion," UPI wrote.

4. "...it is probable that..."
In 1984 Robertson published a book called *Answers to 200 of Life's Most Probing Questions*. This quote is taken from the question (on p.1) "Why is there suffering in the world?" Publisher: The Christian Broadcasting Network, Inc.

5 "I do not need to..."
This Bush utterance was recorded in Bob Woodward's book, *Bush At War* (Simon & Schuster, p. 146, 2002). Pat Robertson's quote: "Even if he stumbles..." is from an interview Robertson did with CNN's Paula Zahn on October 19, 2004.

6. "You say you're supposed..."
Andrew Marshall & Andrew Collier of *The (London) Independent* mentioned this quote in a story about Robertson's attempted partnership with the Bank of Scotland ("One hell of a deal," April 14, 1999).

7. "[I]f he thinks we're trying..."
The Associated Press included this widely reported comment in a February 18, 2006 wrap-up of controversial Robertson statements ("A look at past comments by Pat Robertson" byThe Associated Press).

8. "I don't believe there's..."
CNN captured this Vitter quote in a June 6, 2006 story ("Senate set to reject gay marriage ban"). Stephanie Grace in a June 11, 2006 editorial published in *The (New Orleans) Times-Picayune* wrote, "Me, I find it a little hard to believe that most of Vitter's constituents, staring down another potentially active hurricane season, are spending their time fretting over the prospect of two guys in love..."

9. "I had deep misgivings..."
Robertson uttered this controversial statement on the October 19, 2004 *Paula Zahn Now* show on CNN. Needless to say, the White House disputed Robertson's version of the conversation. "The president never made such a comment," White House press secretary Scott McClellan told CNN on October 21, 2004.

10. "If I heard the Lord..."
Robertson made this prediction on his TV show, *The 700 Club*. The Associated Press wrote about the prediction on May 19, 2006 ("God is warning of big storms, Robertson says").

11. "Christ is head of ..."
This is a fairly famous Robertson declaration. *The Sunday Mail* repeated it in a March 7, 1999 story by Maggie Hall and John Nairn ("Why Barbara, Keith and Balraj won't bank on the man of God who preaches a gospel of hate"). *The National Catholic Reporter* claims that the quote is from a Robertson newsletter ("Robertson should be exposed, not given papal invitation" Vol. 31, No. 43, October 6, 1995).

12. "The only standard journalists..."
This incredibly ironic observation comes from Ann Coulter's book, *How to Talk to a Liberal (If You Must)* (Crown Forum, 2004). *The American Prospect* noted Coulter's observation in a February 1, 2006 piece by Kevin Mattson ("The Book of Liberal Virtues").

13. "That was never in..."
Robertson connected the separation of church and state with the Soviet Union on the January 22, 1995 edition of his program, *The 700 Club*. Americans United for Separation of Church & State reported Robertson's remarks in its April 1996 newsletter *(Church & State, p.10)*.

14. "Take control, Lord..."
Americans United for Separation of Church and State reported this Robertson utterance on an August 3, 2005 posting on their website (www.au.org, "TV Preacher Prays For More Vacancies on U.S. Supreme Court").

15. "The Antarctica ice..."
Media Matters (http://mediamatters.org/items/200605230011) recorded this quote from a May 22, 2006 Rush Limbaugh Show.

16. "There is a woman in Kansas City..."
James Randi recorded this attempt at faith healing in his book *The Faith Healers* (Prometheus Books, 1988). We found the quote via the Los Angeles Times in a May 1, 1988 review of Randi's book by Thomas J. Scheff.

17. "I would like to ask the..."
Dan Henninger spouted this off on *Fox News: The Journal Editorial Report* on June 10, 2006. Henninger began with: "This is a footnote to our gay marriage discussion. A woman in India last week married a snake. And it was done at a traditional Hindu ceremony attended by 2,000 people."

18. "This country is a..."
This quote is from an editorial written by Bill O'Reilly and published in the *New York Daily News* on August 18, 2004 ("Calling Al Franken a satirist is a farce").

19. "Homosexuals are not..."
The Daily Oklahoman recorded this Dobson nugget on October 23, 2004.

20. "But why should we ..."
This unfortunate quote came out of an interview George H.W. Bush and Barbara Bush conducted with Diane Sawyer on ABC News' *Good Morning America* on March 18, 2003. After the former First Lady finished, the former President said to his wife: "You know, you're gonna get us in real trouble. Does that worry you at all?"

21. "I think God's will ... "
Sarah Palin uttered this nugget about God and Alaskan energy policy on June 8, 2008 at the Wasilla Assembly of God. Source: video at wasillaag.net (now removed).

22. "If you go all the way..."
This prediction comes from Pat Robertson's book *Answers to 200 of Life's Most Probing Questions*, which was published in 1984. Publisher: The Christian Broadcasting Network, Inc.